BECAUSE OF THE CROSS

40 DAYS AT THE FOOT OF THE CROSS OF JESUS

JOY MARGETTS

First published in Great Britain in 2025 by Stone Monkhouse Publishing

British Library Cataloguing-in-Publication Data.

A catalogue record for this book is available from the British Library.

Print Book: ISBN 978-1-0683190-2-0

E-Book: ISBN 978-1-0683190-3-7

Books can be purchased from joymargetts.com

Editing and Cover Design by Liz Carter: emcarter.carterclan.me.uk

For Mum,

who led me to the foot of the cross

ENDORSEMENTS

Joy Margetts has a wonderful gift of condensing profound truths into short, snappy devotionals without watering down the message. Although this book is ideal for new believers, it will also remind long-standing Christians of the centrality, relevance, and vital importance of the Cross. It promises to be a huge blessing to all who choose to read it.

Alex Banwell, author of *Just Benny*

I loved Joy's Advent devotional, *Christ Illuminated,* and am delighted she's now written this Lent collection too. Her passion for Jesus, and her desire to unpack the profound and exciting truths of His death and resurrection with all those looking to live out authentic faith in challenging days, are infectious. Beneath its exterior of self-denial and contemplation, Joy demonstrates that Lent carries treasures that will lift your spirit and your heart.

Jenny Sanders, author of *Polished Arrows*

Because of the Cross is a treasure trove of reflections that will accompany readers through the season of Lent, but could be used any time of year. Joy's warm and inviting words will draw you in and give you a place to sit at Jesus' feet and soak in the magnitude of the work of the cross in a new way. Find gold in this beautifully written devotional.

Liz Carter, author of *Catching Contentment* and *Valuable*

CONTENTS

INTRODUCTION

The message of the cross of Jesus is powerful. And it is personal.

What is that message, and what does Christ's death on the cross mean for me? Here and now, as well as in eternity?

I started this exploration as a series of group Bible studies and was soon overwhelmed by all that scripture teaches on the subject. When we truly understand everything Jesus has done for us, and why, it should not only change the way we look at His cross but should also change the way we live now.

I have taken those original group studies and turned them into a daily devotional, in an effort to make the message more individually applicable. Understanding what Christ's death achieved for each one of us personally should encourage and strengthen our souls, bring joy to our hearts, and instil in us a desire to live for the One who gave us His all. So that we can live, fully alive, in the life He died to give us.

My prayer as you go through these daily studies is that you will begin to glimpse the wonder of what Christ's cross accomplished for you. Yes, Calvary was barbaric and messy and horrific, but Jesus endured that because He knew what it would mean for you and me. Because of the cross we can experience a salvation that is rich and full.

This book is perfect for Lent, and that was the season in which it was written. How precious to spend those weeks approaching Easter focusing on the power of the cross! There are 40 studies for that purpose, but this book could be used at any time, at any speed, and by groups as well as individuals.

The devotional is divided into six themed sections. Every day there is a key scripture on which the thought is based, but I would encourage you to read further by opening the Bible to the suggested verses. After each day's reflection, there is a prayer you might like to pray and space to add your own notes or thoughts. Each section ends with a further opportunity for reflection with some questions to aid you.

I have primarily used the New King James Version for scripture references and quotes. I have also used the Passion Translation, as although it might not be a word-for-word translation of the ancient text, and there are some debates over its accuracy, I believe it conveys some sections of the Bible in a fresh and deeply thought-provoking way.

Be blessed as you take time to ponder all that is yours because of the cross of Jesus.

PART 1

BECAUSE OF THE CROSS...

I AM LOVED

DAY 1

GOD IS A GOD OF LOVE

For God so loved the world that He gave His only begotten Son, that whoever believes in Him should not perish but have everlasting life.

John 3:16

Read more: John 3:1-18

This is probably one of the most familiar and quoted verses from the Bible. I have seen it written as graffiti on motorway bridges and even occasionally displayed on football advertising hoardings. Why is it so well-known and used? Because it is the gospel, the good news of Jesus Christ, in a nutshell.

But sometimes our familiarity with the words means we miss the personal and powerful message contained in this verse. It does not say 'For God had so much pity on the world', or 'For God got so frustrated with the world'. It tells us that God so LOVED the world that He gave His only Son.

God has always loved the world and the humanity He created. It was love that made Him create us in the first place. Because He *is* love.[1] The love He has for us is not like the world loves, it is *agape* love – the selfless, unconditional, sacrificial love bestowed on those who do not deserve it. God needed to do something extraordinary and extravagant out of that love. So He gave us Jesus, knowing that His death on the cross was the only way to rescue us and give us back the life we were designed to have. The life that our disobedience had thrown away.

God so loved the world… that He didn't think twice. You may think of Him as angry, distant, uncaring, but He is not. He loves mankind. Out of that heart of love, that ocean of lovingkindness,[2] He gave His only Son so that all who believe in Him can live eternally with Him. He wants to be with you forever! He loves you that much.

PRAYER: Thank You, God, that You are love, and that everything You do and are comes out of that love. Love created me to know You. Love drew me to You. Love provided the way for me to live with You forever.

Thank You for the cross, and for loving the world, loving me, so much that You gave Your Son for us. Help me to live in the reality of the enormity of Your love, knowing that nothing I ever do will change the love You have for me.

---

[1] 1 John 4:8

[2] Psalm 143:8

I stand at the foot of the cross today
and know that God is Love.

DAY 2

JESUS LOVES US

… And walk in the way of love, just as Christ loved us and gave himself up for us as a fragrant offering and sacrifice to God.

Ephesians 5:2

Read more: Ephesians 4:17-5:2

This verse comes in the middle of a section of Paul's letter to the Ephesians where he is urging them to walk in a way that both honours and glorifies Christ. It may cost to live the way of love – Jesus walked it, and it took Him to the cross.

We have seen how the cross demonstrates that God the Father loves us, but in offering Himself, God the Son also showed how much He loved us. Jesus loves us – we who struggle sometimes to live as the new creations He made us. We who struggle to 'put off… the old man'.[3] How easy

[3] Ephesians 4:22

it is to not tell the truth, to speak unkind words, to let anger and bitterness settle in our hearts, to be unforgiving towards others, and even to take what does not belong to us.[4]

Yet still Jesus loves us. He gave Himself as a sacrificial offering on our behalf, and it was a sweet-smelling offering – God approved. The cross demonstrates to us the depth of Jesus' love. He gave us the perfect example of how to walk in love, demonstrating it through His life on earth and ultimately through His death. He was willing to give His life for us, however undeserving we might have been and still are.

Jesus' walk of love took Him up Calvary's hill. So, for us, walking in love might also mean dying – dying to self. He did it willingly because He loved us. Are we willing to follow His lead?

PRAYER: Thank You, Jesus, that You loved us so much that You were willing to offer Your life as a sacrifice for our wrongdoing. As I consider what it cost You to give me new life, help me to put aside sin and selfishness so I can walk in love towards those around me.

Thank You that You gave us the ultimate example of what walking in love looks like. You loved us even when we were lost in our old nature. You still love us when we mess up. Give me Your grace to love others, even when I don't like their behaviour. Show me what it means to love like You do.

---

[4] Ephesians 4:25-32

I stand at the foot of the cross today and know that Jesus gave Himself out of love for us.

DAY 3

JESUS LOVES HIS BRIDE (THE CHURCH)

Husbands, love your wives, just as Christ also loved the church and gave Himself for her.

Ephesians 5:25

Read more: Ephesians 5:25-33

You might have heard this verse read at weddings and it is often used to teach the principles of Christian marriage. With the emphasis on husbands and wives, however, perhaps what this verse says about the enormity of what Christ did for the church can be easily overlooked.

Jesus loved the church, His bride,[5] so much that He gave all of Himself for her. He did that to sanctify her – to cleanse her, to make her into a bride worthy to stand by His side for eternity. His death provided the way for her to become holy and pure, as He is.

[5] Revelation 21:2

A man might choose a woman to be his bride because he loves her. You would hope so! He might want to share all he has with her, serve her, and even lavish her with gifts to prove his devotion. Our bridegroom was so passionately in love with His bride-to-be that He was willing to do everything He could to make her His. Whatever the cost. And it meant that He had to give everything – He gave His very life for her.

How much the Saviour loves us! How awesome a thing it is to be a part of His bride. To know that, in order to join Himself with us forever, He was willing to endure the cross. He could do no more to prove His devotion, and it was all out of a desire to be with us, however unworthy of that love we might feel.

The call on husbands to love their wives self-sacrificially is a tough one. To have the example of what Christ did for His bride certainly puts it into perspective. But that call to love like He did is not just on husbands – or even men! It is on us all as His bride. He has washed and cleansed us, and He is continuing to sanctify us – day by day making us more like Him. So, as we become more like Him, then He will enable us to love as He does. To love Him, our bridegroom, as He deserves to be loved, but also to love others as He commands.[6]

PRAYER: Thank You, Jesus, that You were so entranced by us, so in love with the bride that we would become, that You thought us worth it. Thank You for willingly giving all of Yourself for us.

---

[6] John 13:34

Help me to always remember how much You love Your bride, the church, and, loving You first, help me to love the people of Your bride. Even when it might cost me.

I stand at the foot of the cross today and see how in love He is with His bride.

DAY 4

JESUS LOVES ME

I have been crucified with Christ; it is no longer I who live, but Christ lives in me; and the life which I now live in the flesh I live by faith in the Son of God, who loved me and gave Himself for me.

Galatians 2:20

Read more: Galatians 2:16-21

At the end of Paul's declaration about what Jesus has done to transform his life – how faith in Christ has propelled him to live sold out for Him – he puts it all down to one thing: Paul's reason for putting his old life behind him, for choosing the life of faith, is the revelation that Jesus, the Son of God, **loved him** and gave Himself for him.

Was Paul at the foot of the cross when Jesus died? We don't know. Was he one of Jesus' friends or followers at that point? Definitely not. He was a Pharisaic Jew who would later go on to violently persecute Christians. Yet still, Paul can look back and cry with faith, 'Jesus died for me because He loved me!'

We have already seen that Jesus went to the cross because He loved us and loved the bride, His church. Let's make it even more personal. We can cry with Paul, 'He died for me because He loved *me*!'

Do you ever doubt Jesus' love for you? Perhaps you feel unlovely or unlovable? Perhaps you feel you have let Him down? Perhaps you compare yourself with others and think He can't possibly love you as much as He loves them? Think again.

The cross cries out to your heart – JESUS LOVES YOU.

Jesus loved Paul, the Christian-slaughtering persecutor, and died for him. He looked ahead and thought Paul was worth it. He looked ahead at you and thought you were worth it, too. The cross was for you. You can look to the cross and know how much He loves you. We all need a deeper revelation of what that truly means.

PRAYER: Thank You that You love me, Jesus. Thank You that You love me even when I fail You, even when I am not as Christ-like as I want to be. Still You love me.

Let my life be one of gratitude – that I might be willing to crucify the things of my flesh to live a life that celebrates You and Your love. Forgive me for ever doubting Your love for me.

I stand at the foot of the cross today and see how much He loves me.

DAY 5

I DON'T HAVE TO EARN HIS LOVE

But God demonstrates His own love toward us, in that while we were still sinners, Christ died for us.

Romans 5:8

Read more: Romans 5:5-11

The cross is how God demonstrated His love for us. Whenever we doubt that He loves us, we just need to look to the cross of Christ – as we saw yesterday. And this verse tells us something else powerful: God did not wait for us to be deserving, to *earn* His goodwill; that would be an impossible ask. We were still lost in our sin without Him when He stepped in. It was *while* we were still sinners that Christ died for us.

This is important because we can get so tied up with trying to make ourselves worthy of God's love! That is not what He requires. We can do nothing to earn our salvation; Jesus did it all. His love for us is not dependent on how well we behave, what we achieve, or how religiously we serve. You might feel you have to do things to make people like you or even love you. You might feel you have to prove yourself worthy of the affection of others. But you never have to do that with God. He died for you when you were in your most helpless, hopeless, and ungodly state. He cannot love you any less than He did then – and still does now.

If you ever need proof of this, read Romans 5:8 again and look to the cross. The great demonstration of the Father's love was that when we least deserved it, He gave Jesus to die for us.

PRAYER: Thank You, Father, that I don't have to earn Your love. That the cross of Jesus shows me You love me, even when I don't feel I deserve it.

Let my desire to live for You, to serve and obey You, come from my love for You and gratitude towards You rather than any motive to earn Your approval. You cannot love me any more or less than You already do. And, when I do mess up, help me to run to You for forgiveness, in full assurance that You love me still.

I stand at the foot of the cross today and know that I can't ever do enough to earn His love.

DAY 6

I AM ACCEPTED

... To the praise of the glory of His grace, by which He made us accepted in the Beloved. In Him we have redemption through His blood, the forgiveness of sins, according to the riches of His grace...

Ephesians 1:6-7

Read more: Ephesians 1:3-14

Within us all is the deep need for acceptance. Our children grow up trying to fit in, and that can lead to dangerous and unhealthy subjection to peer pressure. The compulsion is to conform to the things the world deems important, rather than to live under the truth of what God says. Youngsters want to be accepted because the alternative is to be different from the crowd, and to be different can make you a target. It is so sad when young people grow up taking their sense of identity from what others pressure them to be.

But even as adults we seek acceptance too. We don't want to be rejected or feel left out. We may be less driven to change ourselves according to the expectations of others, but we do want to be accepted for who we are. Everyone needs to feel they belong.

In these verses God tells us an extraordinary truth; He has 'made us accepted in the Beloved'. In other words, He loves and accepts us in the same way as He loves and accepts the Beloved One, Jesus Himself.

I don't have to work to be accepted by God. I can come to Him just as I am and know that He accepts me. Knowing this truth – knowing how He loves and accepts me – should quieten my soul against the need to fit in with the world's expectations. My identity is in the fact that I am 'in Him' and sealed for all eternity as His – to bring praise and glory to Him.[7]

PRAYER: Thank You, Father, that I am accepted. I am drawn in, given a place in You. I know where I fit in, because of Your love for me. Jesus, You made it possible for me to know acceptance because You were willing to give Yourself for me. Thank You that I am Yours, for all eternity.

Thank You, Father, that You look at me with the same love as You have for Jesus, Your Beloved Son. Help me to understand the enormity of that and to take my identity from who You say I am.

[7] Eph 1:12-14

I stand at the foot of the cross today and know that I am fully accepted.

DAY 7

I AM A CHILD OF GOD

Behold what manner of love the Father has bestowed on us, that we should be called children of God!

1 John 3:1

Read more: Romans 8:14-17

The love God has for us is not some nebulous, hard-to-grasp concept. God loves us like a perfect Father loves His children. His love is fierce, protective, and unconditional. It looks past failings, it bears with pain, and it can't be switched off.

Many of us who are parents, grandparents, godparents, aunts or uncles, may be able to relate to loving a child this way. We want to do all we can to ensure they are safe, protected, provided for, and secure in our affection. This is an imperfect representation of how God the Father loves His children. In our broken world, you may never have experienced such love from a human parent, but that is the love God has for you.

That love motivated God to seek us, save us, and draw us back to Him. He desperately wanted His children back from where they had wandered.[8] He wanted His children to be free to live life as they were created to live. He wanted a fully restored relationship with us.

Through the cross, He made that possible. He lavished His unconditional love on us so that we could be His sons and daughters. In Him, we are 'joint heirs with Christ',[9] part of His family, filled with His Spirit, with all rights of access and privilege. And He has so much more that He wants to give us – including an eternal inheritance.

The relationship He was looking for was never one of master and slave, but of Father and child. He wants us to have full access to Him and to live in the truth of our sonship.

PRAYER: Thank You, Father, that I can call You Father! Thank You that Your love is so fierce and unrelenting that You gave everything to win me back to You. Thank You that Your love still pursues my heart. Thank You for what the cross accomplished.

Now I am adopted into Your family, I can enjoy all the rights of sonship because of the love that You lavish on me. I am fully accepted, filled with Your Spirit, heir of every spiritual blessing in Jesus,[10] *and protected and provided for, for eternity. I have free access to come to You at any time, without fear, and know You only have the best for me in answer to my prayers.*

---

[8] Luke 15:11-32

[9] Romans 8:17

[10] Ephesians 1:3

I stand at the foot of the cross today and know that I am a child of God.

DAY 8

I AM HIS FRIEND

Greater love has no one than this, than to lay down His life for his friends.

John 15:13

Read more: John 15:9-17

Jesus is in the upper room with His disciples. He knows He will soon die, but they still don't understand that He is leaving them, despite all the times He has told them. The teaching He gives in the last few hours before He leaves them is so important – these are the things He wants them to recall, particularly over the next few distressing days when He will be taken from them and they will believe Him gone forever. He wants them to know, as they sit around that last supper table, that they are His friends.

More than just disciples or followers: friends. Friends worth giving His life for.

The truth is that Jesus laid down His life for many who weren't His friends, yet. He knew, as He gave Himself to that cruel death, that in the days, weeks, and centuries to come, many of those who were and would be His enemies would look to His death and, in faith, turn to Him. His death would turn many enemies into friends.

Do you see yourself as His friend? It is easy to understand why Jesus would address the men and women he had journeyed years with as friends. But what about you and me?

I believe Jesus' words in John 15 echo down the centuries to us. We are His servants (v15), but He tells us that if we seek to follow His commandments (v14) and walk close to Him, learning from Him, and coming to understand the Father's will, then we are also His friends. Friends that He chose, that He will cause to bear fruit (v16), and that He loves. Friends that He was willing to give His life for.

PRAYER: Thank You, Jesus, that You call me friend. Thank You that You demonstrated the greatest love of all by giving Yourself for me on the cross, even when I was Your enemy – so I could become Your friend.

Help me to follow Your lead, to hear You, to understand what You are doing, and to love others as You have commanded. You who demonstrated the greatest friend love of all.

I stand at the foot of the cross today and know that He calls me friend.

DAY 9

HIS LOVE COMPELS ME TO LOVE

This is love: He loved us long before we loved him. It was his love, not ours. He proved it by sending his Son to be the pleasing sacrificial offering to take away our sins.

Delightfully loved ones, if he loved us with such tremendous love, then "loving one another" should be our way of life!

1 John 4:10-11 TPT

Read more: 1 John 4:7-21

God did not start loving us as a response to us loving Him. That is often how human relationships work. The wonderful man who became my husband definitely loved me before I loved him! The way he showed his love for me was a good part of what attracted me to him and how I came to eventually return his love.

God loved us first. When we didn't even know Him, let alone love Him, He made a way to save us. He didn't wait for us to show any affection towards Him, not even the slightest inclination of our hearts. His love for us is so all-encompassing, pure, perfect, and unconditional, that it holds nothing back. He could not help loving us because, as 1 John 4:8 tells us, 'He *is* love.' And 'love is of God' (v7) – He is the source of all love.

We love, and know what love is, because He is love. The ability to love others, even those who are difficult to love, is a sign that we live in Him. He has not only given us the finest example of how to love unconditionally, but He has also given us what we need to love others – His love abiding in us through His indwelling Spirit (v13).

Because He loves us, because He is love, then in Him and through Him we can truly love one another – whether or not we are loved in return.

PRAYER: Thank You, Father, that You are love, that You are the source of love, and that You loved me before I loved You. You love because that is what You do, who You are.

Thank You that, in giving Jesus, You have given us the greatest example of what it means to love self-sacrificially. Enable us to love, God, as You love, even when it costs us. Then we will live in perfect harmony with You, fully loved and able to fully love, by the power of Your Spirit.

I stand at the foot of the cross today and see how Your love compels us to love.

DAY 10

LOVE LOOKS LIKE SOMETHING

By this we know love, because He laid down His life for us. And we also ought to lay down our lives for the brethren.

1 John 3:16

Read more: 1 John 3:10-23

I love how The Passion Translation puts 1 John 3:16:

> 'This is how we have discovered love's reality: Jesus sacrificed his life for us. Because of this great love, we should be willing to lay down our lives for one another.'

The world is looking for real, authentic love. The kind of love that doesn't let you down, fade over time, change or morph into something else. Real, dependable, unchanging, unconditional love. At the cross, we are faced with the reality of real love. This is how we come to discover, understand, and know what real love looks like.

I may say that I love my family, my children, my friends, the people I do church with, my neighbours, and my dog! But would I be willing to lay down my life for them? Is that what God is asking me to do? It may be. Yet the emphasis of 1 John 3 is not necessarily us laying our physical lives down – dying for those we love – but rather a willingness to lay down what we have to bless others in need (v17). To relinquish the right to hold on to what we have been given.

Love should look like something. Jesus' death was a visible expression of His love for us. Our love for one another has to be more than words – it demands a willingness to be self-sacrificial, generous, and responsive to the needs of others; to show real love practically. God promises to meet *our* needs if we do what pleases Him, and part of that is to obey His commandment to love one another. (v22 -23).

PRAYER: *Thank You, Jesus, for showing us the reality of true love and what it looks like to love. You have left us such an amazing example of self-sacrificial love. Help me to be willing to let go of the things I have and own, to lay them down, when I see the needs of others. To love in deed as well as in word.*

I stand at the foot of the cross today and know that real love looks like something.

REFLECTION

BECAUSE OF THE CROSS... I AM LOVED

The cross of Jesus declares YOU ARE LOVED.

Christ's cross reveals the heart of the Father towards His children. We can sit securely in that love, take our identity from how He sees and adores us, and go through life with all its challenges reassured that His love is unconditional and eternal. And we can love others with His help.

It is easy to think about what the cross of Christ accomplished in terms of our salvation, and we will move on to those truths, but we must never forget that it was, and is, His love for us at the heart of it all.

How can I ever doubt that God loves me, personally, when all I need to do is look back to Calvary?

PAUSE

What has impacted you most as you have followed through this section of devotional thoughts?

Has anything come alive for you in a new way?

Have these truths changed the way you think about God? The death of Jesus? Loving others? Yourself?

Take time now to ponder the enormity of God's love for you. How will you respond?

PART 2

BECAUSE OF THE CROSS...

I AM FORGIVEN

DAY 11

MY SINS ARE FORGIVEN

In Him we have redemption through His blood, the forgiveness of sins, according to the riches of His grace.

Ephesians 1:7

Read more: 1 John 1: 5-2: 2

Forgiveness isn't easy – being able to release offence, let go of resentment, walk away from vengeance. As we go through life, we are hurt by people many times. Sometimes the actions and words of others cause us unimaginable pain. God calls us to forgive, but that can feel impossible. He knows that, and He offers us a measure of His grace to enable us to forgive others when it is hard. His grace towards us is so rich, so immeasurable, and He gives us the ability to extend grace to others.

But think for a moment. Don't you think our sin and our rebellion hurt Him? He had every right to be offended and to seek reparation, and yet instead, Jesus went to the cross to bear the punishment for all we have done wrong. He took that pain so we can both be forgiven and walk in forgiveness. God wants us to be free – of our own burden of guilt, and from carrying unforgiveness towards others, which can become such a destructive thing.

The passage in 1 John 1 reminds us that we need forgiveness. Even as Christian people, we can still sin. We can still do things that hurt and offend Christ. 'Walk in the light,' the writer urges us (v7). Keep walking close to Jesus, and your offences – those wrongs that Jesus died for – will come into the light, so you can continue to walk free. None of us are without fault, but there is always forgiveness on offer. All we have to do is acknowledge our wrongdoing and receive what He offers.

When we come to the cross of Christ for the first time, when we acknowledge His death was for us personally, repent, and ask for forgiveness, then it is a done deal. Your sins, past, present, and future, are all forgiven. But He asks us to walk in the light of that, to be aware of when we sin and keep short accounts with Him. Out of the riches of His grace, there is always forgiveness. Always. So, shame has to go. Guilt has to go. He bore it all so that we can walk free and forgiven.

PRAYER: Thank You, Jesus, that You didn't baulk at the cost of forgiving me. When I struggle to forgive others, remind me of what it cost You to offer me forgiveness. And how full and free that forgiveness is, in You.

Give me the grace to forgive others, and give me the grace to walk in the forgiveness You have for me. Help me to walk in Your light and be quick to confess my failings to You, so I can continue to walk free from guilt and shame as You want me to.

I stand at the foot of the cross today and receive free and full forgiveness.

DAY 12

MY SINS ARE FORGOTTEN

As far as the east is from the west,
So far has He removed our transgressions from us.

Psalm 103:12

Read more: Psalm 103

When it comes to forgiving others, we might be able to with God's help, but it isn't always easy to forget the hurt done to us. Over time the pain from the memory might fade, but it might always colour our opinion of that person. And you can be sure that the enemy will bring those things to our minds whenever he wants to create division and disharmony.

Does God remember our sins? Well, this scripture from Psalm 103 seems to imply that He doesn't. How far is the east from the west? It is an immeasurable distance. Keep heading east around the globe, and you will never actually reach west! There is nowhere you and I can go to find what God has removed from us. He is so full of mercy and grace towards us (v8) that the things we should deserve punishment for (v10) He forgives and forgets.[11]

As far as God is concerned, once we have come to the cross, repented of our wrongdoing and received His forgiveness, then our sins are gone. So why do we go looking for them? Guilt and shame can prod us to revisit our past, but as far as God is concerned those things have been removed from our copybook. Let's stop looking for what He has forgotten and rejoice that our forgiveness is full and free in Him!

PRAYER: Thank You, God, that my sins are gone! With You, forgiving is also forgetting; my slate is wiped clean. I have nothing to answer for. Thank You for that total grace gift of forgiveness.

Help me to walk in it, not remembering what You have forgotten, not looking again for the things I am ashamed of but that You have already dealt with. Help me to discern when the enemy of my soul is bringing things to mind that will hurt me and my relationship with others. Help me to bring those things to You.

---

[11] Hebrews 8:12

I stand at the foot of the cross today and rejoice
that my sins are gone.

DAY 13

I AM JUSTIFIED

Much more then, having now been justified by His blood, we shall be saved from wrath through Him.

Romans 5:9

Read more: Romans 3:19-26

What does it mean to be 'justified'? One way I have heard it described is easy to remember and says it all: 'Just as if I had never sinned.'

Imagine a habitual offender being brought to court to ensure the charges against him are answered. The list of indictments is long. But when that list is handed to the judge, he looks at it and with one action wipes it clean. As there are no longer any charges, the prisoner is set free; he has nothing left on his account to answer for.

This is justification. This is what Jesus' death and forgiveness offer us. God is the judge, and as this verse tells us, sin makes Him angry. He will sit in judgement, but when we approach the judgement seat with our long list of wrongdoings, by the blood of Jesus and our faith in Him, the slate will be wiped clean. Case dismissed. We are declared 'not guilty'.

Romans 3 reminds us that not one of us is sinless (v23), none of us is completely innocent. We might try to justify ourselves: 'I am not that bad!', 'I tried to be good', 'Look how many good things I have done'. But self-justification isn't enough (v24).

Only through God's grace, and by Christ's shed blood, are our sins 'passed over' (v26). And then we no longer have anything to answer for. To Him, we are completely innocent.

PRAYER: Thank You, Jesus, for taking the punishment for my sin. You were judged guilty so that I can be judged not guilty. Thank You that in You I am justified.

Forgive me if I ever try to justify myself. In the light of what it cost You, help me to live thankful that although I am never good enough in and of myself, Your death on the cross declares me innocent. You did it all; the case against me has been dismissed.

I stand at the foot of the cross today and know that His blood declares me innocent.

DAY 14

I AM REDEEMED

... Being justified freely by His grace through the redemption that is in Christ Jesus,

whom God set forth as a propitiation by His blood.

Romans 3:24-25

Read more: Hebrews 9:11-15

Because of the cross, we have been justified – declared innocent – but we have also been redeemed, *'the redemption that is in Christ Jesus'*. To redeem something means to buy it back, to pay the redemption price to release something or someone back into our possession. Christ paid the ultimate ransom to buy us back – to redeem our lives from slavery to sin, from certain death. He wanted us that much! His blood pays for our freedom, and we willingly become His possession when we accept that He died for us.

There is another important word in this verse. 'Propitiation' means 'to appease or turn away wrath'. God was and is angry at sin, and yet so in love with sinners that He provided a human 'mercy seat' in Christ Jesus. Sinners in the Old Covenant would come with their offerings to a physical mercy seat, to find forgiveness. Hebrews 9 tells us that under the New Covenant, animal sacrifices are no longer needed. Jesus has not only become the new High Priest (v11), but He also became the once and for all sacrifice (v12).

By shedding His blood, Jesus has not only redeemed us but has become the place of mercy, where God's anger is turned away – the mercy seat that we can openly approach and the seal of our eternal inheritance. There is no more need for any other sacrifice – except perhaps our own lives, given back to him in living thankfulness.[12]

PRAYER: Thank You, Jesus, that the cross justifies but also redeems me. Thank You that You loved me and wanted me back, so much so that You willingly paid the costliest of ransoms for me. You have set me free from slavery to sin and death, and I am forever Yours. By choice, I come to the mercy seat that is your cross and find eternal life in You.

Help me to willingly give my life as a living sacrifice to You.

[12] Romans 12:1

I stand at the foot of the cross today and know that there is always mercy in You.

DAY 15

I AM MADE RIGHTEOUS

For He made Him who knew no sin to be sin for us, that we might become the righteousness of God in Him.

2 Corinthians 5:21

Read more: Romans 5:12-21

Adam sinned – we know the story of the Garden of Eden[13] – but what Adam didn't know at the time was that his one act of disobedience would bring a curse on all mankind. Sin – the innate desire to act against the will of God, to choose self over others, to satisfy the desires of our flesh over the longings of our spirits. Sin, with all of its ramifications – death, suffering, a breakdown of intimacy with God.

We were created in God's image, to be perfect like Him, and sin came and marred that image. We are still seeing the

[13] Genesis 3

effect of Adam's sin in our world and lives today. But God had a plan, from even before Adam fell, whereby one perfect, sinless Man would put things right – through an act of selfless obedience to God, in the giving of His life. Adam's act of disobedience brought judgement and condemnation to all. Jesus' act of obedience extends grace and justification to all.

Can you even imagine living life perfectly? To go through your day without a wrong thought, cross word, or complaint? To never watch, read, or listen to anything you know is ungodly? To never covet or get jealous of others, engage in gossip, or listen to lies? Most of us aren't what the world would consider wicked or evil. We might have done things we are ashamed of in the past, but most of us still struggle daily with the temptation to give in to the desires of our flesh. We sin.

Jesus 'knew no sin'. He lived a perfect life, never giving in to temptation, and yet He died a criminal's death. He never sinned[14] but went to His death without fighting back. He died a righteous man. He took our sin on Himself, bearing it in His body,[15] and took the punishment we deserved.

The righteous One died the sinner's death to make us righteous. In Jesus we are declared righteous – God looks at us and sees Jesus. In this life, He gives us the power to live more righteously[16] by the power of His Holy Spirit, and we will be made fully perfect when we go to be with Him.

---

[14] 1 Peter 2:22

[15] 1 Peter 2:24

[16] 1 Peter 2:24

PRAYER: Thank You, Jesus, for giving us the supreme example of what living righteously looks like. Thank You that You lived a perfect life and were still willing to die a criminal's death so I could be made righteous. Made to look like you.

Thank you that out of your love and grace you provided a way for us to be free of Adam's curse, to be made righteous before you, to exchange death for life. Thank you that the process of being made righteous is ongoing in my life, by the sanctifying work of the Holy Spirit. Help me to live in the power You have given me, the power to live for righteousness.

I stand at the foot of the cross today and know that He sees me as righteous.

DAY 16

I AM CLOTHED WITH SALVATION

I will greatly rejoice in the Lord,
My soul shall be joyful in my God;
For He has clothed me with the garments of salvation,
He has covered me with the robe of righteousness.

Isaiah 61:10

Read more: Isaiah 61:1-7

Clothes are good. They keep our bodies warm and protected against the elements and against shame. They cover our nakedness. Clothes can also be used to express our identity. How we dress might reflect our age, our character, our social status, or our creativity. We might even have to dress in a certain way for work or school, in order to belong.

The clothes God offers us do all the above. 'The garments of salvation' and 'the robe of righteousness' cover our nakedness and shame. They are our protection against the enemy and the effects of sin. They give us our identity. We belong to Jesus, purchased by His precious blood. We are His beloved prodigals, who have returned home to be clothed in rich robes that declare we are His sons and daughters.[17]

These clothes are God's gift to us. He has taken our filthy rags,[18] our attempts to live righteously, and has exchanged them for the perfect robes only He can give.

What does it mean to be clothed with salvation? Isaiah 61:1-7 is full of clues. Salvation is a message of hope to the needy, healing for brokenness, freedom, comfort, beauty for ashes, and joy for mourning. It is also a garment of praise that declares we are rooted in Him, bearing the fruits of righteousness[19] to glorify His name. He exchanges our shame for honour and offers us everlasting joy.

PRAYER: Thank You for my new clothes, God. Thank You that I no longer have to wear filthy rags or mourning clothes. Thank You that Your righteousness covers my shame and gives me a new identity in You.

Thank You for all that my salvation means. Help me stay rooted in You, bearing fruit that honours You, always wearing my garment of praise.

---

[17] Luke 15:22

[18] Isaiah 64:6

[19] Galatians 5:22-23

I stand at the foot of the cross today thankful
for my garments of salvation.

DAY 17

I AM NO LONGER CONDEMNED

There is therefore now no condemnation to those who are in Christ Jesus, who do not walk according to the flesh, but according to the Spirit.

Romans 8:1

Read more: Romans 8:1-11

Because of the cross, God has justified us, declared us innocent, clothed us in Christ's righteousness, and forgiven and forgotten our sins. We have no charge to answer! No one can condemn us to death or punishment, because Jesus has made us His. So, when we hear the voice of condemnation, what do we do with it? With that voice in our head that tells us we are worthless because we messed up? That tells us we are a failure, a not good enough Christian?

The Holy Spirit convicts,[20] but God never condemns us. He might make us feel uncomfortable, aware of our sin, our wrong choices, but that is so we can respond, repent, and move on, knowing that every time we are sorry, He forgives us. The condemning voice is never His.

We have an enemy who loves to make us feel condemned. He knows that if he can get us to feel unworthy, useless, or a failure, we may find ourselves believing those lies and living under their power. God wants us to live as victorious, righteous sons and daughters of the King, heads held high – even if we do still slip up at times.

So, don't listen to self-condemnation. Don't entertain those thoughts or give them a voice; don't empower them. He has declared you innocent – look to Him.

When Satan tempts me to despair
And tells me of the guilt within
Upward I look and see Him there
Who made an end to all my sin.[21]

PRAYER: Thank You, Jesus, that Your death on the cross declares me innocent. Thank You that putting my trust in You means I am no longer condemned. I don't have to believe the lies that tell me I am not good enough.

Thank You, Holy Spirit, for Your work in my life, making me conscious of my wrongdoing and gently guiding me to repentance. Thank You that there is always forgiveness when I

[20] John 16:8
[21] *Before the Throne of God Above*, Charitie Lees Smith (1841-1923) Public Domain

am truly sorry and that You give me strength to grow in grace and learn from my mistakes.

I stand at the foot of the cross today and know that any voice of condemnation is a lie.

DAY 18

I CAN WALK IN FORGIVENESS

And be kind to one another, tenderhearted, forgiving one another, even as God in Christ forgave you.

Ephesians 4:32

Read more: Matthew 18:21-36

The Parable of the Unforgiving Servant, which Jesus told in Matthew 18, is a very powerful story that resonates with us and is deeply challenging. But it amazes me that Jesus told this story before He went to the cross. He told it knowing how much it was going to cost Him to cancel our debt, to forgive us for all that we had done against Him.

We live on the other side of the cross, so this story should impact us even more. We can identify with that first servant, who has just had the debt he could never pay cancelled. His master, out of compassion, lets him go free. As we have seen, through the work of the cross we too can walk free. God has dealt mercifully with us, wiping away our offences and giving us a fresh start.

How it must hurt Him, in the light of what He has so selflessly done for us, when we fail to walk in forgiveness towards others. But it doesn't just hurt Him; it hurts us too. Unforgiveness is so harmful. In Matthew 18:34-35, Jesus warns us that unforgiveness will put us in the place of torture. I personally don't believe God punishes us for not forgiving others, but that unforgiveness in and of itself leads to torture of heart and mind.

Holding things against others worms away at us until bitterness takes root, our peace is stolen, and relationships are irrevocably broken down – including our relationship with our Heavenly Father. *Don't come to my altar; don't come with your offering of worship,* God says, *if you are in conflict with someone else.*[22] *Be merciful, as I am merciful.*[23]

Forgiving others might be hard. It might cost us. But it cost Jesus everything to forgive us. Our only reasonable response, with His help, is to extend grace to others. To continue to walk in the freedom He died to give us.

PRAYER: *Thank You that I have been shown such mercy and compassion, that my debt has been cancelled because You died for me. And I can walk free, fully forgiven. Help me never forget what it cost you to forgive me.*

[22] Matthew 5:23-24

[23] Luke 6:36

As I walk in my freedom, help me to also walk in forgiveness towards others. Help me remember how important it is to You, and how life-giving it is to me, to be quick to forgive. Gift me with a measure of Your great compassion and mercy so I can let go of offence, even when it costs me.

I stand at the foot of the cross and know you call me to forgive.

DAY 19

I AM THE REASON FOR HIS JOY

… Looking unto Jesus, the author and finisher of our faith, who for the joy that was set before Him endured the cross.

Hebrews 12:2

Read more: Isaiah 53:6-12

This is an astounding scripture. It says that in approaching His death, Jesus could see beyond it to the joy that would be His after His agony was done. Isaiah 53 tells us that He would know deep satisfaction for what His work had achieved (v11) and that He was looking ahead to His seed (v10). What was the 'seed' the writer is referring to? Who would be the reason for Jesus' joy and satisfaction? The 'seed' is those who would come to Him and find their life in Him. Those who would become His sons[24] and heirs. He went to the cross for the joy of knowing you and me, of being back in relationship with us.

[24] Galatians 3:26

Do you know that you bring Him joy, that He delights in you?[25] He loves that You are His. He knew that His death would justify you and bring you back to Him. It made it all worth it.

Jesus loved His disciples on earth,[26] but when He went to the cross it wasn't just for them; it was for us too. Jesus endured the cross and despised the shame – He conquered the humiliation – because of the joy that was to come. He did not become distracted or wearied from His purpose but stayed steadfast to the end. Because He wanted us so much!

PRAYER: Thank You, Jesus, that I am Your joy! That being in relationship with me brings You delight. Thank You that You endured, persevered, and conquered death because You wanted me to know You. You wanted us to be together forever.

Help me to persevere, to not grow weary in running my own race of faith, even when it gets tough, as I look to You, Jesus, as my perfect example.

[25] Zephaniah 3:17
[26] John 13:1

I stand at the foot of the cross today and delight that I am the reason for Your joy.

REFLECTION

BECAUSE OF THE CROSS… I AM FORGIVEN

The cross of Jesus declares YOU ARE FORGIVEN.

There is so much to our salvation, and it is all because Jesus was willing to go to the cross in our place. The sinless One became sin so that the guilty can be declared innocent. The forgiveness God offers is full, free, and complete. A done deal. He sees us as righteous in Christ, clothed in the robes of salvation He has given us.

We are no longer condemned, no longer guilty. We can live free from shame, free to live for Him, always learning what that looks like. One day we will be fully like Him, sanctified and made holy. We can walk in forgiveness towards others.

Jesus did not turn back but endured the pain and shame of the cross, because He wanted us to be free. He wanted us. We are His joy.

PAUSE

What has impacted you most as you have followed through this section of devotional thoughts?

Has anything come alive for you in a new way?

Have these truths changed or enhanced the way you think about forgiveness? Justification? Guilt and condemnation? Forgiving others?

Take time now to ponder the enormity of the forgiveness that is yours through Christ. How will you respond?

PART 3

BECAUSE OF THE CROSS…

I AM RECONCILED

DAY 20

I AM RECONCILED TO GOD

... That God was in Christ reconciling the world to Himself, not imputing their trespasses to them, and has committed to us the word of reconciliation.

2 Corinthians 5:19

Read more: 2 Corinthians 5:14-21

I wonder what the word 'reconciled' means to you: what imagery does it evoke? The dictionary describes it as 'the restoration of friendly relations'.[27] When we have fallen out with someone, especially when that breakdown in relationship has lasted for some time, we can long for a reconciliation. Perhaps you have witnessed a reconciliation between friends or family members? It is a powerful thing.

A few years ago, I heard an amazing woman speak about her work promoting reconciliation between the warring

[27] Oxford Languages (Google.com)

factions in Rwanda, the Hutu and the Tutsi, after the civil war had ended.[28] If you remember the Rwandan genocide, and what those rival people groups did to one another, you will realise that any degree of reconciliation would be huge. It took much grace, forgiveness, and willingness to forget the wrongs done. To put the past behind them in order to move forward in peace. Remarkably, with God's help, that happened in many places.

Jesus did the same for us on the cross. Out of His wealth of grace, God has forgiven our 'trespasses' and forgotten the wrongs we have done against Him. He wants reconciliation. He wanted it so much that He provided the way, through Christ's death, for us to be at peace with Him. We are reconciled – back in peaceful relationship with Him, forever.

PRAYER: Thank You, God, that you did not want to continue in broken relationship with us. Thank You that You provided the way for us to be reconciled, through Jesus. Thank You that I am forgiven, my past forgotten, and I am back in peaceful relationship with You, forever.

Help me to carry the ministry of reconciliation to others. To show them that You want to heal relationships with them also. Help me always seek to restore the broken relationships in my life, with the help of Your great grace.

---

[28] Rhiannon Lloyd. Read more in her book, *'Fire Lilies: Finding Hope in Unexpected Places'*

I stand at the foot of the cross today and know that my relationship with God is fully restored.

DAY 21

FROM ENEMIES TO FRIENDS

For if when we were enemies we were reconciled to God through the death of His Son, much more, having been reconciled, we shall be saved by His life.

Romans 5:10

Read more: Colossians 1:19-23

We were God's enemies, alienated from Him because of our sin.[29] It was while we were in that state that Christ died for us. Why? Because God didn't want us to be His enemies; He wanted us to be His friends. Jesus died to save us from the consequences of our wrongdoing and to give us eternal life. But He also died because He wanted us to be close to Him; reconciled, never to be at odds again. He wants a loving, trusting, intimate relationship with us, where we enjoy His company and He enjoys ours.

[29] Col 1:21

Those Rwandan warring factions we read about yesterday may have made peace, but I wonder how many true friendships sprung from those reconciliations. We can forgive those who have hurt us, and even try to forget; we can come to a place of peace with them. But being friends is something deeper still. Friends are those we hold close. Friends love, trust, and rely on one another; they share life, know each other well, and enjoy being together. They share secrets, hopes, and dreams; they sharpen, encourage, and spur one another on.

As we saw earlier, if we trust and follow Jesus, He calls us His friends.[30] His death accomplished that. We are now friends with God. The things that alienated us from Him, our sinful hearts and minds, have been dealt with. We have gone from hostile enemies to the closest of friends. And even more than friends – He has made us His sons and daughters. From enemy to child? That is some reconciliation!

PRAYER: Thank You, Jesus, that I am no longer your enemy. That all hostility between me and God has been dealt with. I love that You call me friend and that I am Your child. Thank You that I can entrust myself to You, and live close to You, knowing how much You love me.

Help me be a true friend to others. To put aside the things that might cause division, to forgive, and to build trust. To love as You call me to love. Thank You for those You have put in my life who are my true friends.

[30] John 15:15

I stand at the foot of the cross today and know that He wants me to live close to Him.

DAY 22

I AM RECONCILED TO OTHERS

But now in Christ Jesus you who once were far off have been brought near by the blood of Christ.

Ephesians 2:13

Read more: Ephesians 2:11-22

Ephesians 2 tells us that we were once 'aliens and strangers' (v11), outside the covenant promises of God, without hope and without God in this world (v12). But through his shed blood, Jesus, the peace-bringer, has broken down the wall of separation (v14), not only between us and God but between us and others.

Paul is writing to Gentiles (non-Jews) here. Under the Old Covenant, God's promises of protection, blessing, forgiveness, and life were only available to those who lived under the Law given to Moses – the people of Israel. Jesus' death brought in a new way, a New Covenant,[31] sealed in His blood, by which all people, both Jew and non-Jew, could come into a life-giving relationship with God the Father. The heart of this passage is that our ethnicity, where we come from, who our family is, or our position in society no longer matters – because in Christ we are all one.

Christ's death not only reconciles us to God but also provides a way for us to be beautifully connected with those who, outside of Christ, might have been our enemies. When we are restored to God, we also become restored to one another. All prejudices, all lines of division, are rubbed out. All of us have the same direct access to Him, through Jesus. All of us are part of the same body. All of us are part of a holy temple, built on the foundation of Christ, in which God's Spirit dwells.

There is no 'stranger' or 'alien' in Him. No division, except of our making. We are citizens of heaven, drawn together to live for Him and His kingdom. No lesser, no greater, all one.

PRAYER: Thank You, Jesus, that in Your death You not only restored my relationship with God but also provided a way for me to be one with those whom I might have considered my enemies.

Thank You for the body of believers, the living temple built on the foundation of what You did for us, and that I have been welcomed to be a part of it.

---

[31] Luke 22:20

Where I have caused or perpetuated division within Your body, forgive me. Help me see what a gift it is to be reconciled to others, to be one in You.

I stand at the foot of the cross today and know I am part of a body of believers, all one in God.

DAY 23

I HAVE CONFIDENCE TO APPROACH HIM

Therefore, brethren, having boldness to enter the Holiest by the blood of Jesus, by a new and living way which He consecrated for us, through the veil, that is, His flesh…

Hebrews 10:19-20

Read more: Matthew 27:45-54

God's desire was always to live with His people, to be close to them, but in His holiness that could not be. The tabernacle that God instructed the children of Israel to build, and later the temple that replaced it, were both designed to host God's presence: a means by which He could live among them and yet apart. He could be approached, but He dwelt in the Holy of Holies, a separate space, cut off from the people by a thick heavy veil or curtain. Only the high priest could enter the Holy of Holies, once a year, on behalf of the people, and it was a terrifying experience. Sin cannot approach the Holy.

And then Christ came and went to the cross. God dwelt among men in human form, making Himself approachable, and then offered up His life as a once and for all sacrifice. As He died, the temple veil was torn in two, from top to bottom. No human hand did that. God did it. That symbol of separation between a Holy God and a sinful people was ripped away forever.

We no longer have to fear approaching God. We don't have to go through a complicated series of sacrifices and offerings, or indeed need a human high priest. We don't have to step through a visible veil; Jesus is the veil in person, and His torn flesh is the means by which we now enter the Holy of Holies. We can come boldly, knowing we have been made holy and righteous in Him. Jesus has made possible what God has always wanted. Because of the cross, we can live close to Father God. We can approach Him freely, without fear or shame, with confidence and boldness.

PRAYER: Thank You, Jesus, that Your torn flesh is my way into the presence of God, that at Your death all physical separation between me and my Father was removed. Thank You for Your righteousness that makes me both worthy and bold to approach You and to be close to God.

Thank You, God, that You want to live in close relationship with me. It has always been your deepest desire and why the cross was necessary. Help me have confidence in approaching You. I can come to You just as I am, and I am always welcome in Your presence.

I stand at the foot of the cross today and see how much He wanted to be close to me.

DAY 24

GOD LIVES IN ME

Or do you not know that your body is the temple of the Holy Spirit who is in you, whom you have from God, and you are not your own? For you were bought at a price; therefore glorify God in your body and in your spirit, which are God's.

1 Corinthians 6:19-20

Read more: John 14:15-18

Christ's death reconciles us to God, bringing us into close relationship with the One we were once at enmity with. But it goes further still. We can be with God, because of Jesus' sacrifice, but it has also made a way for God to be with us and *in* us. When we believe in our hearts that Jesus has died for us and accept God's gift of forgiveness and new life, then by His Spirit God comes to live in us. This was what Jesus promised His disciples in John 14 – another One, just like Him, who would be with them and in them (v18). This promise is for us too.

What a wonderful comfort that He lives in us! Our helper,[32] guide, comforter, and friend. He chooses to dwell in us and promises us that He will never leave us,[33] ever. It is such an amazing mystery that the One who created the universe would want to make His dwelling place inside our hearts!

It is also a challenge. He wants us to live led by the Spirit who dwells inside us and not according to the desires of our flesh. This is how we become more like Him. As Paul says in the verses we read, we need to remember how much a price was paid for us to live a better life. We are called to live lives that glorify Him, which means we must 'flee' or run away from the things that would trap us into sinful behaviour. He has given us His Spirit so we do not have to do this alone. We need to listen to Him and be in tune with Him so that we take seriously the cost He paid to give us new life.

PRAYER: Thank You for Your Spirit, who lives within me, and that I am never alone because You are both with me and in me. Thank You, Jesus, that You were willing to pay the cost to bring me back in to relationship with You and the Father.

Help me to live in the Spirit – seeking to be guided in all things by the One who dwells within me. Help me to turn my back on the sins of the flesh and live to glorify You.

---

[32] John 14:16
[33] John 14:18

I stand at the foot of the cross today and know
He has come to dwell within my heart.

DAY 25

THERE IS JOY IN HIS PRESENCE

You will show me the path of life;
In Your presence is fullness of joy;
At Your right hand are pleasures forevermore.

Psalm 16:11

Read more: Psalm 16

A few days ago, we thought about how Jesus went to the cross because of the joy of having us back in relationship with Him. But His death gives us access to joy as well; joy unlike anything else. Joy: a deep inner peace and contentment in every circumstance, as opposed to fleeting happiness.

God is the source of true joy, and it's only in His presence we experience 'fullness of joy'. Why is His presence the place for us to find complete contentment? Well, I believe we were created to be with Him; that is the purpose of our existence. We were designed to live close to Him, so that is why all our deepest longings are met in His presence.

Psalm 16 encourages us to celebrate this – the amazing inheritance we have in Him (v6), all that being in relationship with Him provides for us now and in the future. We can be glad and rejoice, finding hope for the future (v9). This is life in abundance,[34] being fully satisfied with His fullness and drinking of His fountain of life.[35] This is the joy He wants us to know, and it is ours if we make it our purpose to live close to Him.

Life here on earth can bring its joys: our children, our families, the blessings of friends, accomplishments, holidays, celebrations. But those joys are often fleeting, as life also brings pain and sorrow. Because of Jesus, the way has been made for us to rest in God's presence, to know the joy He gives, even in the midst of difficult times. And that is not just as we walk this 'path of life' but for 'forevermore' (v11) in His presence. Because of the cross.

PRAYER: Thank You, Father, that You are the source of true joy and I can find full contentment living close to You. Thank You, Jesus, for making the way possible for me to never have to be separated from God and the life He gives, now and for eternity.

Help me to look to You as the source of my contentment, God, especially when the joys of life are fleeting. Teach me to be glad and rejoice in every circumstance because I know You. I was made to be with You.

---

[34] John 10:10

[35] Psalm 36:8-9

I stand at the foot of the cross today and know my joy is found in Him.

REFLECTION

BECAUSE OF THE CROSS... I AM RECONCILED

The cross of Jesus declares YOU ARE RECONCILED TO GOD.

How does it make you feel that God wanted to be with us so much? That Jesus' cross made a way of reconciliation so that we could move past all the things that separate us, and live close to Him as we were designed to?

God can turn enemies into friends – He did it for us. We were alienated from Him, but now, because of the cross, we can approach Him boldly and come to Him just as we are, always accepted.

The relationship between us and God is so close now He lives within us by His Spirit. He chooses to dwell with us and in us. Living close to Him is where we find true contentment, whatever life throws at us. He is our source of lasting joy.

PAUSE

What has impacted you most as you have followed through this section of devotional thoughts?

Has anything come alive for you in a new way?

Have these truths changed the way you think about God and you? You and others? Approaching God? True joy?

Take time now to ponder the truth that God wants to be with you. How will you respond?

PART 4

BECAUSE OF THE CROSS...

I AM HEALED

DAY 26

DEATH AND DISEASE ARE DEFEATED

Surely He has borne our griefs
And carried our sorrows;
Yet we esteemed Him stricken,
Smitten by God, and afflicted.
But He was wounded for our transgressions,
He was bruised for our iniquities;
The chastisement for our peace was upon Him,
And by His stripes we are healed.

Isaiah 53:4-5

Read more: Isaiah 53

We have seen and meditated on how Christ's death dealt with our sin. As Isaiah says, 'He was wounded for our transgressions, He was bruised for our iniquities.' We have seen how the cross has made peace between us and God: 'The chastisement for our peace was upon Him.' But Christ's death for us did yet more; it not only defeated sin, but also conquered the effects of sin and its curse – death, and every other foul result of the fall of man – including sickness and pain.

In Isaiah 53, that powerful prophetic outcry that looked forward to the cross, we read that He bore our 'griefs' and carried our 'sorrows'. Those two words have complex meanings and could be translated in other ways, as indeed they are in other Bible versions. 'Griefs' can also be translated as 'disease, sickness, illness', and 'sorrows' as 'pain, suffering'. When the gospel writer Matthew quotes Isaiah 53:4 he says this:

> 'He Himself took our infirmities and
> bore our sicknesses.'[36]

Matthew saw the connection as He watched Jesus heal the multitudes from physical ailments. Jesus literally took their infirmities away.

Isaiah says, 'By His stripes we are healed.' Does this just apply to the healing of our souls? No, I don't believe so. Every lash of that whip that scourged[37] His back provided a way for every type of healing. Will we all receive healing in this lifetime? Or will we only see full freedom from pain in heaven? We will come to those big questions, but for today, let us just acknowledge what Matthew understood: there is healing in the work of the cross.

PRAYER: Thank You, Jesus, for enduring the pain of the cross to provide a way for me to be free of suffering. Thank You that You

---

[36] Matthew 8:17
[37] John19:1

were stricken so I don't have to be. Thank You that there is healing in the cross.

Help me to believe You can heal and that You have made the way for me, and those I love, to be made whole in every way. Help me to trust You about what healing might look like, but never to deny that You are the healer.

I stand at the foot of the cross today and see the wounds that bring healing.

DAY 27

JESUS HAS OVERCOME

... How God anointed Jesus of Nazareth with the Holy Spirit and with power, who went about doing good and healing all who were oppressed by the devil, for God was with Him.

Acts 10:38

For this purpose the Son of God was manifested, that He might destroy the works of the devil.

1 John 3:8b

Read more: Romans 8:31-38

The verse from Acts 10 states clearly that Jesus' ministry to heal and set free was in direct opposition to the work of the evil one. 1 John 3:8 tells us that the purpose of Christ's coming, through His death and resurrection, was to destroy the works of Satan once and for all.

Sickness is not from God. It is from the pit of hell. The things that cause suffering in this life are a direct result of sin's curse, the fallen world we live in. In God's heavenly kingdom, there will be no sickness because there is no sin and no curse there – just as in the Garden of Eden before mankind fell. It is the enemy of our souls who seeks to steal, kill, and destroy,[38] not God. His will is for us to have life, in abundance.

When Christ died and rose again, He defeated the eternal power of Satan. He defeated sin, death and ALL the works of the evil one. He conquered, He overcame. He is the victorious One.

We have questions – why does God allow suffering? Why doesn't He heal everyone? I don't have easy answers to those questions. Jesus told us that our lives in this world would not be free from tribulation,[39] trouble, and pain. Yet the truth still stands – He has overcome it all. We are on the winning side, more than conquerors.[40] Whatever life throws at us, nothing can separate us from Him, His power, and His love.[41]

PRAYER: Thank You, Jesus, that You are the victorious One, that You have forever defeated the power of Satan. Thank You that sickness and suffering do not come from You; You want me to have full and abundant life.

Help me to believe that You have the power to heal. Thank You that whatever I have to endure You will be with me, and give me victory in You.

---

[38] John 10:10
[39] John 16:33
[40] Romans 8:37
[41] Romans 8:39

I stand at the foot of the cross today and know that Christ has overcome the works of the evil one.

DAY 28

HEALING OF HEARTS

He has sent Me to heal the brokenhearted.

Isaiah 61:1

Read more: Isaiah 61:1-3, Luke 4:16-21

Alongside physical sickness, emotional and spiritual pain are also direct results of sin and our fallen nature. Diseases of the mind, dysfunction in our emotions, broken spirits, anything that is not perfect health and wellbeing. All these 'sorrows' and 'griefs' Jesus carried to the cross.[42]

No one can truly understand the mental, emotional, and spiritual pain that Jesus went through as He went to His death. We get a glimpse of its intensity in the Garden of Gethsemane, where He pleaded with the Father and sweat drops of blood. When He desperately needed the company of His disciples, and they abandoned Him. And at the

[42] Isaiah 53:4

cross, when He had to endure mocking, jeering, and insults. As He hung in agony, still the crowd taunted Him. Most of His loved ones deserted Him; some betrayed and denied Him. It even felt to Him that God had abandoned Him. It was not just physical pain that Christ endured on the cross.

He bore these things for us. Why? So that we could be healed of them. His very purpose in coming to live among humanity, and in dying for us, was to heal the broken-hearted. He declared it of Himself when He quoted Isaiah's prophecy in Luke 4. He came to comfort the grieving, to console the desperate, to exchange joy for despair, to create a people set free to praise Him.[43] He can do that for each one of us.

PRAYER: Thank You, Jesus, that You were prepared to endure emotional agony as You went to the cross for me. Thank You that You understand what it feels like to be broken-hearted, alone, and grieving. Thank You that in the work of the cross there is healing for all brokenness.

Help me to come to You when I am struggling, to accept Your peace and joy in exchange for my sorrow and despair. Show me the areas of my life where You want to set me free.

---

[43] Isaiah 61:2-3

I stand at the foot of the cross today and know
He understands sorrow and grief.

DAY 29

HEALING IN HEAVEN

And God will wipe away every tear from their eyes; there shall be no more death, nor sorrow, nor crying. There shall be no more pain, for the former things have passed away.

Revelation 21:4

Read more: Revelation 21:1-7

I don't know about you, but one of the things I am looking forward to in heaven is a new body! The promise is that there will be no more pain, suffering, sorrow, or grief there. The 'former things' will be gone. Sin will be gone, death and Satan defeated forever. And all the effects of the curse on mankind will be finally done with. Revelation 21:6 declares, 'It is done,' echoing the words that Jesus cried from the cross with His dying words, 'It is finished.'[44] Christ's death on the cross defeated it all.

[44] John 19:30

In heaven, we will walk completely free from ill-health. We will never know grief, loss, or heartbreak again. I can't wait! Life will be perfect, as God intended it, joy-filled because we are with Him. Revelation 21 tells us that He is coming back for His adorned bride,[45] ready to make us His forever, and that He will wipe away our tears of sorrow. The only tears in our eyes as we encounter Him will be tears of joy!

'God Himself will be with them and be their God.' (Revelation 21: 3) We will be a people flowing with His life, those who have overcome and will enjoy Him forever. He will make everything new, our bodies included.

PRAYER: Thank You, Jesus, that our greatest joy in heaven will be to be with You. Thank You that there will be complete and perfect healing in heaven, as all pain and sorrow are forever done with.

Thank You that I am part of Your bride and that, by Your sanctifying work in my life, You are making me beautiful, ready to meet You. Thank You that although I might have to live with suffering in this life, I can look forward with hope to what lies ahead of me in heaven with You.

---

[45] Rev 21:2

I stand at the foot of the cross today and look forward to an eternity of perfect healing.

DAY 30

HEALING ON EARTH

And these signs will follow those who believe: In My name they will cast out demons… they will lay hands on the sick, and they will recover.

Mark 16:17-18

Read more: Matthew 10:1-8

In Matthew 10 we read how Jesus sent out the 12 disciples, giving them His authority and saying to them,

> 'Heal the sick, cleanse the lepers, raise the dead, cast out demons. Freely you have received, freely give.'[46]

In Luke's gospel, we see Jesus send out 70 more disciples, commissioning them in a similar way – to heal the sick.[47]

---

[46] Matthew 10:8

[47] Luke 10:9

Jesus promises in Mark 16 that all those who believe in Him will have the power to heal in His name. To 'those who believe' – this includes all of us who follow Jesus – He promises Holy Spirit empowerment. It is not that we can heal others in and of ourselves, but that Jesus, by His Spirit, gives us His power and authority to do so. What was demonstrated by the apostles in the New Testament is also available to us today.

Healing is part of the work of the cross, but it is God's gift to give. He gives 'gifts of healing',[48] and He gives those gifts in His time and His way. He calls us, however, to live for His kingdom. Jesus taught us to pray, 'Your Kingdom come, Your will be done, on earth as it is in heaven.'[49] As we have seen, there is no sickness in heaven, so in demonstrating His kingdom here on earth, we can expect to see God heal.

It is His will to heal, in the timing and way He decides, but He wants us to be the means to see people receive gifts of healing. It might be a challenge to our faith, but as those who believe, it is right to pursue healing for ourselves and for others.

PRAYER: Thank You, Jesus, that You give us Your authority and power to pray for the sick in Your name. Thank You that the cross has enabled Your kingdom to become more of a reality on earth. Thank You for Your gifts of healing.

Give me the courage to pray for others who need Your healing, in faith and in Your name.

---

[48] 1 Corinthians 12:9

[49] Matthew 6:10

I stand at the foot of the cross today and have faith that He can heal.

DAY 31

HIS HEART TO HEAL

And when Jesus went out He saw a great multitude; and He was moved with compassion for them, and healed their sick.

Matthew 14:14

Read more: Mark 1:40-45

In Matthew 14, we see Jesus doing what He loves to do. Even though He was exhausted and likely grieving for His cousin, John the Baptist; even though the crowds had found Him in His place of rest and solitude,[50] His compassion for them did not waver. He worked all day, and it was a large crowd, a multitude of more than 5,000 people.[51] Still His love and care for them propelled Him to heal.

[50] Matthew 14:13

[51] Matthew 14:21

In Mark 1:40, the leper came to Jesus and asked Him if He was willing to heal him. Again, Jesus was moved with compassion and reached out to touch him, saying, 'I am willing, be cleansed.'[52] God has great compassion for us in our suffering. He loves to heal. He is willing to heal. Those are truths we must believe.

Why aren't all our prayers for healing answered? There are no easy answers to this question, but I don't believe it is because God doesn't care or is unwilling to heal. We must trust God's sovereignty and leave the questions with Him, exchanging our discomfort for His peace. The reality is that Jesus' life and death were all about healing: spiritually, physically, and emotionally. He still loves to heal and is still willing to heal.

PRAYER: Thank You, Jesus, for the compassion You showed to those who were in need when You walked on the earth. Thank You that You were always ready and willing to heal those who came to You. Thank You that You still offer healing today.

Help me trust You with the answers to my prayers for healing but never believe that You do not care. When I pray, 'Your will be done,' help me to remember that You are not willing for me to suffer.

---

[52] Mark 1:41

I stand at the foot of the cross today knowing that You are willing to heal.

REFLECTION

BECAUSE OF THE CROSS… I AM HEALED

The cross of Jesus declares THERE IS HEALING.

The cross of Jesus is all about healing. Spiritual healing, of course, but also emotional and physical healing. We may not see the fulfilment of all the perfect healing the cross promises until eternity, but that doesn't mean there is no healing this side of heaven.

There are lots of difficult-to-answer questions around healing, but these truths remain: God heals, He loves to heal, and He is willing to heal. He gives gifts of healing and calls us to walk in His authority and pray with faith for others to be healed.

Jesus has overcome all the works of the evil one by His death on the cross. Sickness doesn't come from God; it is a result of the fallen world we live in. All will be made right one day, and we will be perfectly free from all pain when we go to be with Him.

PAUSE

What has impacted you most as you have followed through this section of devotional thoughts?

Has anything come alive for you in a new way?

Have these truths changed the way you think about healing for yourself? Healing for others? What God feels about healing? Your authority in Him to pray for healing?

Take time now to ponder the truths that God loves to heal and is willing to heal. How will you respond?

PART 5

BECAUSE OF THE CROSS...

I AM VICTORIOUS

DAY 32

FREED FROM SLAVERY TO SIN

... Knowing this, that our old man was crucified with Him, that the body of sin might be done away with, that we should no longer be slaves of sin.

Romans 6:6

For sin shall not have dominion over you, for you are not under law but under grace.

Romans 6:14

Read more: Romans 6:15-23

In our humanity, we were born into slavery to sin. Sin has the power to control us, to drag us into doing, saying, and thinking things that can do real damage. To ourselves, to others, and even with long-reaching consequences for generations to come. Because Adam sinned, we are born into sin.[53]

[53] Romans 5:12

The cross provided a way out – freedom from slavery to sin. Jesus took our sin on His own body,[54] and by doing so defeated its power. If we give ourselves to Christ, our old man is done with – put to death – we no longer have to live as slaves to sin. In Christ, we lose the desire to sin as His righteousness calls us to a better way. As His Spirit within guides and sanctifies us, we gain the power to resist temptation and to live, not completely sinless, but not governed or controlled by sin.

We can be victorious over the temptation to sin. It is what Jesus wants for His followers, and what His death paid for. That means we can live less selfishly, more attuned to the needs of others, and more aware of how our behaviour affects them.

A slave has no control over themselves or what they are forced to do. A freed man can decide to live free!

PRAYER: Thank You, Jesus, that Your death made the way for me to be free from the power of sin. You paid the price, and You gave me Your Spirit, to empower me to resist temptation. Your cross calls me to live victoriously.

Help me to walk free from temptation, and when I do sin, to be swift to repent and acknowledge my mistakes so You can help me move on from them.

[54] 1 Peter 2:24

I stand at the foot of the cross today and know
I am free from slavery to sin.

DAY 33

DEAD TO SIN, ALIVE IN CHRIST

... Reckon yourselves to be dead indeed to sin, but alive to God in Christ Jesus our Lord.

Romans 6:11

Therefore, if anyone is in Christ, he is a new creation; old things have passed away; behold, all things have become new.

2 Corinthians 5:17

Read more: Romans 6:1-11

Our theme today follows on from yesterday and is laid out in the first part of Romans 6. Death frees someone from sin, because dead people can't sin (they can't do anything!) (v7). Christ's death on the cross defeated both the power of physical death and of sin (v8-9). Just as Jesus was raised from the dead to resurrection life (v4), so we can be made alive 'to God' in Him (v10-11).

If we are in Christ, we can, in effect, die to our old selves: die to sin. He died for our sin, and we are raised to a new life in Him. Does that mean we can live sinless lives on earth? Not completely, no. But it does mean we can live more inclined to not sin. We have a new nature that He has given us; we are a new creation in Him.

Jesus' death defeated the *power* of sin in our lives. The 'old man',[55] that old way of living, where sin reigned in our lives, has been put to death in Christ. The old has passed away and the new has come. But we still have the choice to give in to sinful desires or not.

He has made us alive in Him and given us a new life where that desire to sin should be diminished. We are still required to resist temptation but have His Spirit within to give us the power to do so. We also have a desire to live for Him, in a way that pleases Him, and He is continually sanctifying us by His work in our lives. We live in the glorious grace that He gives us. We are alive, not just in our mortal bodies, but in our spirits as His Spirit breathes His life into us.

PRAYER: Thank You, Jesus, that Your death has the power to put to death my sinful nature. That I can be a new creation in You. Thank You that by Your Spirit You have breathed new life into me, and I can live in a way that glorifies You, in gratitude for what You have done for me.

Help me to seek to live for You, knowing that I have Your Spirit within me to help and guide me. Thank You for the new life that awaits me in eternity.

[55] Colossians 3:9

I stand at the foot of the cross today and know
I am a new creation in Him.

DAY 34

A DESIRE TO LIVE FOR HIM

... Present yourselves to God as being alive from the dead, and your members as instruments of righteousness to God.

Romans 6:13

He died for all, that those who live should live no longer for themselves, but for Him who died for them and rose again.

2 Corinthians 5:15

Read more: Romans 6:12-14

When you think about the cross – about what Jesus did for you, the sacrifice He paid, the pain He endured – I wonder how your heart responds. The whispered words 'thank You' don't seem enough, somehow, do they? What can I do or say to show Jesus how much His death means to me? Here is the answer.

Out of gratitude, out of love for Him, with the cost of our salvation always in our minds, we give ourselves wholly back to Him. As willingly as He gave Himself for us, so we give over our lives to Him. As Romans 12:1-2 tells us, we 'present' ourselves, our bodies, as 'living sacrifices' to Him – our 'reasonable service'. The only reasonable response to what He has done for us is to choose to walk in a way that pleases Him, victorious over sin, covered by His grace. That is our act of worship.

His death gives us life, and that life belongs to Him. Our bodies, minds, gifts, and abilities are all for Him. The life He died to give us should be lived to honour Him!

PRAYER: Thank You that Your death gave me life, Jesus, and that You willingly gave Yourself for me. I love You, and I want to worship You by giving my life back to You.

Help me to live for righteousness, victorious when tempted to sin, aware of Your grace, but also aware that it is my choice to live in a way that honours You and Your death for me.

I stand at the foot of the cross today and choose to live for Him.

REFLECTION

BECAUSE OF THE CROSS… I AM VICTORIOUS

The cross of Jesus declares SIN HAS NO POWER TO CONTROL YOU.

The death of Jesus gives us the chance for a new life, a new way of living not controlled by the power of sin or our sinful natures. He has made the way for us to live differently. We can know victory over temptation because He defeated sin and death by His death and resurrection.

Jesus has overcome the power that sin has to control us. He has given us His Spirit to help us resist temptation, but it is still our choice whether we live for Him or according to the desires of our old natures.

We will be perfectly sinless one day and completely free from all temptation when we go to be with Him. But here, today, our only reasonable response to all He has done for us is to offer Him our whole lives as living sacrifices.

PAUSE

What has impacted you most as you have followed through this section of devotional thoughts?

Has anything come alive for you in a new way?

Have these truths changed the way you think about sin's power in your life? What having a new nature means? What it looks like for you to offer yourself as a living sacrifice to Him?

Take time now to ponder the truth that you can be victorious over sin because of Jesus' cross, and that He calls you to live for Him. How will you respond?

PART 6

BECAUSE OF THE CROSS...

I AM ALIVE

DAY 35

LIFE IN ABUNDANCE

For God so loved the world that He gave His only begotten Son, that whoever believes in Him should not perish but have everlasting life.

John 3:16

I have come that they may have life, and that they may have it more abundantly.

John 10:10

Read more: John 7:37-39

Jesus' death and resurrection defeated death and the grave. 'Oh death, where is your sting?'[56] we can cry. We don't have to fear physical death if we belong to Him; we know that we have eternal life, that our souls will live with Him for eternity. Because of the cross. But Jesus didn't just die to give us life in heaven. The everlasting life He promises

[56] 1 Corinthians 15:55

begins the moment we put our faith in Him. He wants us to live full, abundant lives here on earth.

Life doesn't feel abundant at times! It can be hard, painful, and challenging. But I don't believe we are supposed to merely endure life on earth whilst looking forward with longing to life in heaven.

Jesus prayed to His Father, 'Your will be done, on earth as it is in heaven.'[57] Heaven is a place of peace and joy, but those things are also available to us now. He wants us to know life that, despite its hardships, can be full of His peace, joy, hope, faith, and yes, blessing! We have so much to be grateful for. He wants us to live victorious, powerful, God honouring, fruit-producing lives. He wants us to know life in abundance.

We can't do any of that in and of ourselves, but His life-giving Spirit is alive inside every one of us who believes. A stream of living water that we constantly need to tap into.[58]

PRAYER: Thank You that Your death, Jesus, not only brought me eternal life but also abundant life here on earth. When things get tough, help me to go back to the source of my life, Your Spirit living within me. Give me Your peace, joy, and hope. Help me live as if heaven were on earth; a victorious, powerful, fruit-producing life.

[57] Matthew 6:10

[58] John 7:38

I stand at the foot of the cross today and know that I have abundant life in Him.

DAY 36

HIS LIFE IN ME

I have been crucified with Christ; it is no longer I who live, but Christ lives in me; and the life which I now live in the flesh I live by faith in the Son of God, who loved me and gave Himself for me.

Galatians 2:20

Read more: Galatians 5:15-26

The new life that is mine in Christ Jesus is a gift. My old life, living in my own strength – making mistakes, enslaved to the power of sin, burdened with guilt and shame – is gone. It lies at the foot of the cross.

The amazing life His death offers is so powerful that death could not hold it captive. If I have given my life to Him, then His powerful resurrection life is alive in me.[59] I am empowered by that life as He calls me to live for Him.

[59] Romans 8:11

He doesn't ask me to do that in my own strength – I need His help to enable me to live a victorious, God-honouring life, here on earth. I can walk in the Spirit and put to death the things of the flesh. He asks me to put my faith in Him and walk closely with Him. As I lean close and listen to His life-giving Spirit within me, I know what choices to make, what things offend Him, and which paths to steer clear of.

The walk of faith is one where I cling tightly to Him, my heart open to Him, full of love and gratitude for what He has done for me, alive in His Spirit. The outworking of that is fruit – lasting spiritual fruit that will bless Him, bless me, and bless others.

PRAYER: Thank You, Jesus, for new life in You. Thank You that You are alive in me by Your Spirit, and that the same power that raised You from the dead can empower me to live a life that glorifies You and produces good fruit.

Thank You that You never ask me to live a holy life in my own strength, but that You have already given me all I need. Every spiritual blessing is mine in Christ Jesus.[60]

[60] Ephesians 1:3

I stand at the foot of the cross today full of His resurrection life.

DAY 37

HIS PRESENCE (FOREVER)

Lo, I am with you always, even to the end of the age.

Matthew 28:20

Read more: John 14:15-24

The last recorded words of Jesus in Matthew's gospel are so comforting. Before He ascended into heaven, He said to his followers, *I might be leaving you physically, but My Spirit, My presence, will never leave you*. Before His betrayal and crucifixion, Jesus had promised the disciples that another 'helper' would be sent to them from the Father.[61] That He, the Spirit of truth, would dwell with them and in them. As His followers today, those who love Him and obey His Word, the promise is ours as well.

As we saw yesterday, He is alive in us by His Spirit. He is forever with us. We never have to be alone again.

---

[61] John 14:16

Sometimes it feels like we are alone. When we are abandoned or misunderstood by others, left alone by the cruelties of life and tragic circumstances. Sometimes just living the life Christ has called us to, can feel lonely and impossibly hard.

However we might feel, the truth emblazoned across the Word of God is that we are *not* alone. We will never have to walk life's tricky path on our own. We may not always understand the circumstances we are having to live through, but still this comfort is ours. Just as Jesus came to be with His disciples in that storm-tossed boat,[62] His presence can bring peace into every storm we face.

PRAYER: Thank You, Jesus, for Your promise to never leave us. Thank You for the comforting presence of Your peace-giving Spirit in my life. When I feel lonely or overwhelmed in life's circumstances, help me fix my gaze on You.

Thank You that Your presence goes with me, all the time, every day, and will continue to until I am with You forever in heaven.

[62] Mark 6:50-51

I stand at the foot of the cross today and know
His presence is with me.

DAY 38

HIS PEACE

Peace I leave with you, My peace I give to you; not as the world gives do I give to you. Let not your heart be troubled, neither let it be afraid.

John 14:27

Read more: John 14:25-27, Philippians 4:6-7

Peace. Our world needs peace so drastically. How we long for conflicts to end, for people to live in harmony, for striving to cease. But the peace Jesus is speaking of isn't that kind of peace. Peace treaties between warring factions don't tend to have long-lasting effects. Another grievance, another act of violence, and suddenly peace is broken. '*Not as the world gives,*' Jesus says.

The peace Christ offers is His eternal peace. One day, everything will be made right in a new heaven and a new earth, where there will be no more wars. That peace is available to us as His followers now. It was His parting, lasting gift to His disciples and to us.

His peace in our hearts comes from knowing that He has all things in His hands. He has promised to be our provider, protector, comforter, and healer. He is our Saviour and deliverer. We can be at peace, deep in our souls, whatever is going on in the world or in our lives, because we can place our hope and trust in Him.

Don't be troubled, don't be afraid, and don't give into anxiety – believe in Him and what He has promised He will do for you. This is the place of peace.

PRAYER: Thank You, Jesus, that the peace You offer is so different from what we understand peace to mean in this world. Thank You that Your peace can never be taken from us, that it is Your eternal gift to us.

Forgive me when I step out of the place of peace; when I allow Your peace to be taken from me and give in to fear and worry. Thank You that You are always there to reassure me and that You will keep every one of Your promises.

I stand at the foot of the cross today
and accept the peace He offers.

DAY 39

HIS STRENGTH

I can do all things through Christ who strengthens me.

Philippians 4:13

Read more: 2 Corinthians 12:7-10

I can do *all* things, Paul declares, with certainty. The word 'can't' is rife in our world. My three-year-old grandson has already learned it and uses it frequently, even when what he declares to be impossible is well within his capabilities. How often does the thing we want to do, or feel we have been called to do, seem too big for us – we just can't see how we could possibly do it?

That is actually a good place to be, because when we realise our human weakness – our frailty, our inadequacies – then we are driven to lean into God's strength.

He is the expert at the impossible. Just look at the resurrection of Jesus! Nothing or no one has more power than He. God has all the strength we need, emotionally, spiritually, and even physically, to live the life Christ's death has purchased for us, and enough grace for us to endure when life is tough,[63] or when we are lacking in any way.

When we realise our own weakness, when we choose instead to lean into Him, then His strength will enable us to do more than we ever thought possible.

PRAYER: Thank You, Jesus, that You promise to meet me in my place of weakness with Your amazing strength. Thank You that You never call me to do anything for You without providing all I need to accomplish it.

Thank You for the joy of knowing my weakness is a good thing if it makes me depend on You more. Forgive me for relying on my own strength when You say to rely on Yours.

[63] 2 Corinthians 12:9

I stand at the foot of the cross today and see
His strength, available for me.

DAY 40

HIS RESURRECTION POWER

Behold, I send the Promise of My Father upon you; but tarry in the city of Jerusalem until you are endued with power from on high.

Luke 24:49

Read more: Acts 4:24-35

The resurrection of Jesus declares His power. Nothing can withstand it, not even death itself. This very power Jesus promised to His disciples is available to us today. The power that raised Christ from the dead is alive and at work within us through His Holy Spirit.

All authority was given to Jesus,[64] and He gives it to us, just as He gave it to His earthly followers. The Holy Spirit descended at Pentecost, and He transformed those He fell upon. That same Spirit lives in us and anoints us to serve;

[64] Matthew 28:18

to complete His commission to 'go and make disciples'[65] and to show His power to heal and transform lives.[66]

God intended that the life Jesus bought for us was to be a life of power. A life that transforms the world we live in and that impacts others for the Kingdom of God. The power to heal the sick, raise the dead, and cast out demons in His name lives within each one of us.

We are called to live lives of abundance, and that includes being fruitful – walking in His authority and power, speaking of Him, and demonstrating that He is real and interested in the lives of the people we meet.

This is the life the cross gives us. Abundant, powerful, victorious, peace-filled, trusting, fruitful, and reliant on His strength, not our own; a life lived in obedience to His call in response to all He has done for us.

PRAYER: Thank You, Jesus, for the cross and the life You died to give me. Help me to live in the abundance of life You have prepared for me. Help me know the power of Your resurrection in all I seek to do in serving You and Your kingdom.

[65] Matthew 28:19

[66] Mark 16: 15-18

Thank you Jesus for the cross and that it stands empty today.

REFLECTION

BECAUSE OF THE CROSS… I AM ALIVE

The cross of Jesus declares YOU HAVE THE LIFE OF CHRIST WITHIN YOU.

Christ's death on the cross, and our acceptance of it, reconciles us to God. He offers us forgiveness, freedom from guilt, and a chance for a new start. His resurrection life makes us alive in Him. His power within us, by His Spirit, empowers us to live abundant lives.

Not only have we been brought near to God, but He has also come close to us – so close that He chooses to live within us. His presence will never leave us; His peace and strength are always available to us.

He calls us to live gloriously victorious lives, whatever circumstances we find ourselves in. His powerful resurrection life is at work within us. We are alive in Him, now and for eternity.

PAUSE

What has impacted you most as you have followed through this section of devotional thoughts?

Has anything come alive for you in a new way?

Have these truths changed the way you think about the Holy Spirit and His life in You? The life He is calling you to lead? The peace and strength He offers?

Take time now to ponder the truth that His resurrection life and power live within you. How will you respond?

ENDNOTE

I hope this little book has encouraged and blessed you.

It may be that, in the course of reading this book, you have found yourself standing at the foot of the cross of Jesus and seeing it clearly for the very first time.

You need to know that there is an invitation being extended to you. God loves You. Jesus wants you to experience all that His death made available for you. He wants you to be free from sin, and guilt, and shame. He wants to heal you from the inside out. He wants to offer you new life, abundant life; His presence, strength, peace, and joy. And most of all He just wants to be with You.

You were created to be with Him, now and for eternity. You are the reason for His joy.

I wonder if you will respond, by kneeling at the foot of Jesus' cross, even today, and offering your life to Him in full surrender? You may be doing that for the first time, or you may feel the need to recommit yourself to Him. Just know that He sees your heart and His arms are wide open, waiting to embrace you.

He surrendered His life for you, to give you everlasting life in Him.

ACKNOWLEDGEMENTS

This book came about because of the loving encouragement of so many.

My church leaders and friends who recognised the gift God had given me to teach His Word and gave me the opportunity to do so.

My praying friends who have stood with me every step of this writing journey.

Publishers who have believed in my ability to write.

My Kingdom Story Writer friends who have read drafts, corrected and challenged, made improvements, prayed and cheered me on. Special thanks to Alex Banwell, Jenny Sanders, and Elizabeth Gyfford.

Natasha Woodcraft, Joy Vee, and Rachel Yarworth for answering countless questions, and being there when I needed you. You gave me the courage to forge ahead with this project.

Liz Carter for doing such a magnificent job in editing and cover/interior design.

My family who love me and put up with all this writing stuff, especially my long-suffering hubby. And my parents – I would never have encountered Jesus at the cross if it hadn't been for them.

For all these, I am so grateful.

But most of all – Thank You, Jesus. For the cross, for the life Your death has given me, and for this opportunity to write about You. Thank You for Your Word, which is the bedrock of my faith and my place of safety. Thank You for this book.

www.ingramcontent.com/pod-product-compliance
Ingram Content Group UK Ltd.
Pitfield, Milton Keynes, MK11 3LW, UK
UKHW041023250225
4745UKWH00019B/58